ANALYZE THE ANCIENTS

ANCIENT
Egypt

Louise Spilsbury

Gareth Stevens
PUBLISHING

Please visit our website, www.garethstevens.com.

For a free color catalog of all our high-quality books, call toll free 1-800-542-2595 or fax 1-877-542-2596.

Cataloging-in-Publication Data

Names: Spilsbury, Louise.
Title: Ancient Egypt / Louise Spilsbury.
Description: New York : Gareth Stevens Publishing, 2019. | Series: Analyze the ancients | Includes glossary and index.
Identifiers: LCCN ISBN 9781538227183 (pbk.) | ISBN 9781538227190 (library bound)
Subjects: LCSH: Egypt--Civilization--To 332 B.C.--Juvenile literature. | Egypt--Antiquities--Juvenile literature.
Classification: LCC DT61.S646 2019 | DDC 932'.01--dc23

First Edition

Published in 2019 by
Gareth Stevens Publishing
111 East 14th Street, Suite 349
New York, NY 10003

© 2019 Gareth Stevens Publishing

Produced for Gareth Stevens by Calcium Creative Ltd
Editors: Sarah Eason and Jennifer Sanderson
Designers: Paul Myerscough and Jessica Moon
Picture researcher: Rachel Blount

Picture credits: Cover: Shutterstock: Jaroslav Moravcik; Inside: Flickr: Horus3: p. 12; Shutterstock: Ewais: p. 4; Bogdan Ionescu: pp. 33, 45; Andrea Izzotti: p. 5; Jsp: p. 29; Maciek67: p. 10; Vladimir Melnik: p. 26; Mountainpix: p. 36; Jaroslav Moravcik: p. 30; R.M. Nunes: p. 11; Pakhnyushchy: p. 25; Peter0808: p. 27; Eric Valenne geostory: p. 24; Repina Valeriya: p. 23; Vladimir Wrangel: p. 13; Wikimedia Commons: p. 37; لا روسيا: p. 9; Osama Shukir Muhammed Amin FRCP (Glasg): p. 16; James Byrum: p. 8; Captmondo: p. 43; Marcus Cyron: pp. 1, 35; Dada: p. 20; Daderot: p. 21; Ismoon: p. 34; Janmad: p. 39; Jastrow (2007): p. 17; Mike Knell: p. 14; LACMA; William Randolph Hearst Foundation: p. 19; Juan R. Lazaro: p. 6; Maler der Grabkammer des Nacht: p. 41; Ad Meskens: p. 18; Andreas Praefcke: p. 38; Rogers Fund, 1915: p. 31; Rosemania: p. 32; Keith Schengili-Roberts: p. 40; Nikola Smolenski: p. 7; The Yorck Project: p. 28; Wknight94: p. 22; World Imaging: p. 42.

Printed in the United States of America

CPSIA compliance information: Batch #CS18GS: For further information, contact Gareth Stevens, New York, New York at 1-800-542-2595.

CONTENTS

CHAPTER 1

The Ancient Egyptians

About 5,000 years ago, the different cities that ran alongside the Nile River in Egypt were brought together as one **kingdom** ruled by one leader—the pharaoh. Ancient Egypt was one of the world's first **cultures** and one of the most famous in history.

On the Banks of the Nile

Egypt is a country in North Africa, where most of the land is desert. The Nile River flows northward through the center of the country. Every year, the river floods its banks, bringing water to the strip of land on either side. The river also washes **fertile** mud onto this area of soil. This allowed the ancient Egyptians to grow crops to feed a growing population. The dark, rich soil around the river was so important to them that the ancient Egyptians first called their country Kemet, which means "Black Land." Beyond the narrow strip of land all along the river where the ancient Egyptians lived lay the deserts where they buried their dead. Beyond that were the cliffs that helped protect ancient Egypt from invaders.

THE RIVER THAT FLOODS
Without the Nile's life-giving waters, the culture of ancient Egypt would not have existed.

An Expanding Empire

The ancient Egyptians conquered other countries and gradually created a huge **empire**. They also developed a highly distinctive culture. They built vast pyramids, **temples**, palaces, and tombs, and produced some of the most splendid paintings and carvings ever seen. Their culture also made great advances in science, technology, and religion. Egypt thrived and was the most powerful nation in the Mediterranean world between 3150 BC and 30 BC. One example of their great skills was the device they built to measure the height of the floodwaters from the Nile River in summer. This helped them figure out how much water they would be able to use when they started to dig and plow their fields in October, when the hot, dry summer season ended.

Three Kingdoms

The ancient Egyptian culture lasted for more than 3,000 years, which is longer than any other **civilization** in human history. Its history can be divided into three main periods: the Old, Middle, and New Kingdoms. The time periods between the three kingdoms were known as Intermediate Periods.

Old Kingdom

During the early period of ancient Egypt, from about 2686 BC to 2200 BC, pharaohs had absolute power. They were believed to be representatives of the gods. A number of **monuments**, such as the Sphinx, and many pyramids were built, mainly at Giza in today's Egypt. That is why this period is often called the Age of the Pyramids. The pharaohs of the Old Kingdom chose Memphis as their capital city. It was located at the meeting point of Lower Egypt and Upper Egypt.

THE MAN IN THE MIDDLE

This painting of Mentuhotep II is from his tomb. This ruler reunited Egypt and became the first pharaoh of the Middle Kingdom.

Middle Kingdom

Mentuhotep II from Thebes defeated the last of the rulers of the Old Kingdom and founded the Middle Kingdom, which lasted from around 2100 BC to 1800 BC. The capital became Thebes and the pharaohs made the god of Thebes—Amun—the most important god. During the Middle Kingdom, ancient Egypt strengthened its armies to protect the land from enemies. During that time, Egypt was divided into districts called nomes. Trade with other countries thrived and there were many developments in art and science. The pharaohs of the Middle Kingdom tended to be buried within tombs that were well hidden, rather than in the towering pyramids of the Old Kingdom.

New Kingdom

The first pharaoh of the New Kingdom and the eighteenth **dynasty** was Ahmose. The New Kingdom, which lasted from about 1500 BC to 1000 BC, was a very successful time for the ancient Egyptians. They conquered new lands and expanded the country's borders. Famous pharaohs of this time include Hatshepsut, Tutankhamun, and Ramses II. Priests became more powerful, and more Egyptians believed in funeral **rituals** for the dead.

A VALLEY FOR KINGS
In the New Kingdom, pharaohs were buried in the Valley of the Kings.

Examining Evidence

One reason people find the ancient Egyptians so fascinating is that we have a lot of evidence about their culture. We know a lot about their pharaohs, their daily lives, what they ate and wore, and how they lived. All this information comes from objects **archaeologists** have discovered and the writings the ancient Egyptians left behind.

Tomb Time Capsules

The ancient Egyptians believed that there was life after death. They buried their dead in the deserts beyond the cities and villages where they lived along the river. With them, they buried all the goods they thought the dead would need in the **afterlife**. These underground tombs are like time capsules. The hot, dry conditions of the desert helped preserve their contents. Materials such as plaster, wood, cloth, leather, skin, and an ancient Egyptian form of paper called papyrus, all survived. The tombs also held a range of artifacts—pots, weapons, and other items recorded on papyrus, which tell us about the ancient Egyptians.

HISTORY DETECTIVES

Archaeologists in Egypt search for evidence from the past in the area surrounding an ancient Egyptian pyramid.

Secrets Revealed

Artifacts found in tombs mostly tell us about powerful leaders because the largest and best-hidden tombs were made for them. These tombs were filled with the most precious artifacts. Scenes of everyday life painted on tomb walls show us how ordinary people lived. One of the most famous tombs belongs to Tutankhamun. The beautiful and expensive golden death mask over his sarcophagus, or coffin, is evidence that he was a pharaoh. Only pharaohs such as Tutankhamun were allowed to wear an image of the cobra goddess, seen below on his crown. The idea was that the cobra goddess would protect pharaohs by spitting flames at their enemies.

ANALYZE THE ANCIENTS

This is the death mask from Tutankhamun's tomb. Based on the information you have learned, can you answer the questions to analyze the ancient Egyptians? Check your conclusions against the Answers section on pages 44–45.

1. When archaeologists found this object, what did it tell them about the person who wore it?

2. The symbol carved into the crown shows a cobra goddess. Why do you think pharaohs chose to wear this symbol?

CHAPTER 2

Who's Who in Ancient Egypt?

Egyptian culture had different levels. At the very top were the gods. Egyptians believed that the gods controlled everything and that it was important to keep them happy. Just below the gods came the pharaohs. Egyptians believed their leaders were gods in human form.

Pharaohs and Dynasties

The pharaoh had absolute power over their people. Not only were they a ruler, the pharaoh was also the high priest of the Egyptians, the empire's most important religious person, the chief judge, and commander-in-chief of the army. A pharaoh usually passed on their power to their son, so ancient Egypt was ruled by a series of dynasties. A pharaoh's wife, or queen of Egypt, was also a powerful ruler.

A FEMALE PHARAOH

Hatshepsut was one of several women pharaohs. To reinforce her power, she ordered that she should be portrayed as a male pharaoh in statues and images.

There were several women pharaohs and rulers, too. Each time a new family took control of the throne and the country, a new dynasty began. During ancient Egypt's 3,000-year history, there were more than 30 different dynasties and more than 170 different rulers.

Some Famous Pharaohs

- Tutankhamun is the best known because of the discovery of his almost-intact tomb containing fabulous treasures. He became pharaoh at the age of 9 in about 1333 BC and ruled until his death at the age of 18.

- Hatshepsut made herself Egypt's first woman pharaoh after her husband died. She ruled successfully between 1473 BC and 1458 BC, leading armies into battle and sending out expeditions to bring exotic goods to Egypt.

- Ramses II ruled from about 1279 BC to 1213 BC. He fought many battles to get new land and created grand buildings, statues, and temples.

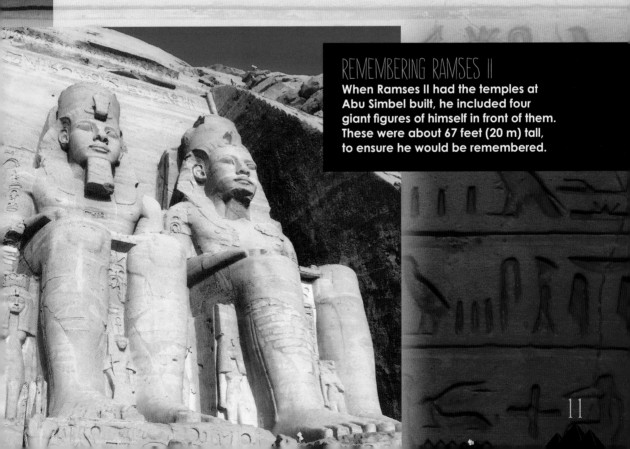

REMEMBERING RAMSES II
When Ramses II had the temples at Abu Simbel built, he included four giant figures of himself in front of them. These were about 67 feet (20 m) tall, to ensure he would be remembered.

Positions of Power

A pharaoh was responsible for their people. To protect them, they had to run an army ready to defend an attack by foreign soldiers or in battles between different regions of Egypt. The pharaoh decided what laws were made. They also owned large warehouses for storing the grain that farmers paid to the pharaoh as taxes. The pharaoh kept the grain safe and would distribute it to feed the people when there were food shortages, such as after a drought. To carry out these duties, the pharaoh had powerful people to help them.

Nobles and Priests

After the pharaoh, the most powerful people were the **nobles** and priests. The nobles worked for the pharaoh or the royal family, often helping govern, or run, the country. For example, a noble who worked as a government official might supervise the preparation of a king's tomb. The nobles also watched over the different nomes, or districts, of Egypt. Priests were responsible for pleasing the gods. Although the pharaoh was the high priest, they could not attend ceremonies all over Egypt. So, different priests carried out the sacred rituals at each temple. The priests enjoyed great power and wealth.

MEASURING THE HARVEST
This painting found on the wall of a tomb shows workers measuring and recording the harvest.

12

A SEATED SCRIBE

This is a sculpture of a seated scribe from ancient Egypt. He is shown at work, holding a partially rolled papyrus scroll in his left hand. His right hand must have held a brush, but that is now missing.

Viziers and Scribes

The vizier was the highest official in ancient Egypt to serve the pharaoh. They were the chief minister of the government, and they ensured that taxes were collected. All the courts in the land had to answer to the vizier. Then the vizier reported to the pharaoh. Scribes were people who worked with the vizier. They could read and write, so they kept government records. They kept records of the crops harvested, figured out the amount of food needed to feed tomb workers, kept accounts, and ordered supplies for temples and for the Egyptian army.

The People of Egypt

Most of the people of Egypt were in either the lower class or middle class. People usually **inherited** the type of job they did. If their father was a farmer, they became a farmer when they grew up, too. If a family saved enough to send a smart son to a school run by priests or scribes, it was possible for him to become a scribe.

The Lower Classes

At the bottom of the social structure were farmers and **slaves**. Farmers grew crops and raised animals, and helped build royal monuments. In times of war, some were forced to become soldiers and fight. They became soldiers of a lower **rank.** Important soldiers might ride chariots, but lower ranks marched for days or weeks to reach the enemy. Many fought wearing just a tunic and a pair of sandals, armed with only a spear. People captured as prisoners of war became slaves. Slaves were forced to work on building projects, and for the pharaoh, nobles, and other powerful people.

BUYING AND SELLING SLAVES
This is a carving of an ancient Egyptian slave market, with slaves from Nubia waiting to be sold. Nubia was a powerful empire between Egypt and Ethiopia that fought Egypt for land.

The Middle Classes

During the New Kingdom, ancient Egypt needed strong, well-trained armies to keep foreign enemies out and to conquer other countries. These soldiers used weapons such as spears, daggers, and swords. During times of peace, soldiers supervised the workers and slaves who were building pyramids and palaces. Other members of the middle classes included skilled workers such as doctors, craftspeople who made jewelry, pottery, and other useful or decorative items, and merchants who sold these goods.

ANALYZE THE ANCIENTS

These depictions of soldiers were found on an ancient Egyptian tomb. Can you analyze the ancients and answer the questions below?

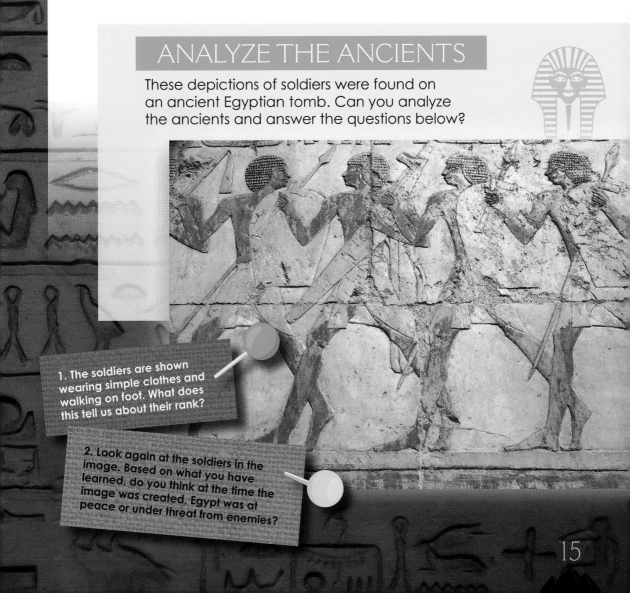

1. The soldiers are shown wearing simple clothes and walking on foot. What does this tell us about their rank?

2. Look again at the soldiers in the image. Based on what you have learned, do you think at the time the image was created, Egypt was at peace or under threat from enemies?

CHAPTER 3

Gods and Beliefs

The ancient Egyptians believed in around 750 different gods and goddesses. Each god had a different role to play in keeping the Egyptians safe and happy. Gods and goddesses had many duties. Some made the Nile flood every year, some kept people safe, and others watched over families or the dead. Some gods were linked to particular towns or parts of the body.

Different Gods

Some gods looked similar to humans, but others were part human and part animal. Animals were chosen to represent the powers of the god. For example, Sekhmet was the fierce goddess of war and battle, so she had the head of a lioness. Anubis was the god of the dead, tombs, and **embalming**. He had a head of a jackal because jackals often roamed the edges of the desert, near where the dead were buried. Priests often wore a mask of Anubis during **mummification** ceremonies. Ra was the sun god. He was the most important god of the ancient Egyptians. The ancient Egyptians believed Ra was swallowed every night by the sky goddess Nut, and was reborn every morning.

DAUGHTER OF RA

The goddess Sekhmet, meaning Powerful One, is the daughter of the sun god Ra. She wears the sun as a headdress and is protected by a spitting cobra.

This illustration from the ancient Egyptian _Book of the Dead_ shows the gods weighing a person's heart to find out whether they were good or bad.

Upper World and Underworld

The Egyptians believed that the gods ruled over Earth where humans lived, which they called the upper world, and the underworld where people went after they died. When a dead person traveled through the underworld, their heart was tested to see if they had led a good life on Earth. If it was found to be pure, they would be sent to live forever in the beautiful heavenly paradise they called the "Field of Reeds." There, they would live the same sort of life they had lived on Earth, so a king would still be king and a farmer would still be a farmer. If a person's heart failed the test, they would be eaten by Ammit, a female Egyptian demon that had the body of a lion and the head of a crocodile.

Ways to Worship

The ancient Egyptians feared many things, such as wild animals, drought, and other natural disasters. They also feared the destruction of the sun. They believed that to stay safe, they had to please their gods and goddesses. To do this, they built beautiful temples in which the Egyptians and their priests could worship and give **offerings** to statues of the gods that lived there.

Inside the Temples

The main gods and goddesses, such as ram-headed Amun, one of the most powerful gods in ancient Egypt, were worshiped in the inner spaces of large temples. The pharaoh and priests prayed and made offerings to gods and goddesses on behalf of the people. Ordinary people did not take part in these ceremonies. Instead, they left offerings of food or flowers in the outer temple. The priests then collected and offered up these offerings.

THE BARK OF HORUS

Inside the temple at Edfu is the sacred bark, or boat, of the god Horus, who chased away enemies of his father Ra.

18

The Power of Amulets

Ordinary people saw the statues of the gods that lived in the temples only when priests paraded them through the streets during processions. They also worshiped some gods in their homes, such as Bes who protected people from dangers such as snake bites and scorpion bites. They could also buy protective amulets, or lucky charms, which were made in the temple workshops. The amulets represented gods, and people believed that they had powers. The Eye of Horus was one of the most popular amulets. Horus was a god of the sky with a head of a hawk. He protected people and especially pharaohs. After one eye was torn out in battle, it was returned to him and became a symbol of good health. Horus amulets were often made with a special blue stone called turquoise, which they believed gave powerful protection against wounds or other attacks.

ANALYZE THE ANCIENTS

This is an ancient Egyptian amulet. Based on what you have read, can you answer these questions about it?

1. What is the symbol on this amulet and what does it mean to the person who wore it?

2. The amulet is made from turquoise. Why do you think people chose this stone to make the amulet?

Making Mummies

The ancient Egyptians believed in the afterlife, so they developed a way to preserve the bodies of their dead for this next stage. This process is called mummification. After a pharaoh died, embalmers worked on their body for 70 days. Only after the pharaoh was successfully embalmed could their family say farewell to them.

The First Steps

The first step in making a mummy was to clean the body carefully and thoroughly. Then, the embalmers removed the liver, lungs, and other organs from the dead body. The brain was removed through the nose by a long hook. Then the body was covered in a type of salt to dry it out. After 40 days, the salt was removed and the body was oiled to keep the skin from cracking. As the body dried out, it lost its shape, so it was stuffed to give it shape again.

WRAPPING A MUMMY

When the mask was removed from this ancient mummy's head, it revealed a sophisticated design formed by the strips of linen wrapped around the face.

GIFTS TO THE GODS

Animal mummies, such as these cats, were made and sold to people who wanted to give them as offerings to gods associated with a particular animal.

The organs that had been removed and dried were now put back inside the body.

Making a Mummy

Next, the embalmed body was wrapped in strips of fine linen cloth, which were painted with liquid **resin** to glue the strips of linen together. While the mummy was being wrapped, a priest read out spells to chase off evil spirits and help the dead person travel safely through the underworld. Embalmers also put amulets between the layers of cloth to protect the body on its journey. Between the hands rested a papyrus scroll with a collection of spells to help the person find their way to the afterlife. Then the body was wrapped in a cloth that was painted with an image of the god Osiris, chief god of the dead and the afterlife, and placed within two coffins. Finally, the completed mummy was sealed in a sarcophagus and placed inside a tomb along with food and drink, furniture, clothing, and other valuable objects for the afterlife.

CHAPTER 4

Pyramids and Monuments

There were many different jobs in ancient Egypt. The ancient Egyptians built enormous stone constructions and monuments, many of which still stand today. Pharaohs ordered huge monuments to be built for everyone to see just how powerful they were. The most famous of these are the mighty pyramids.

Building the Pyramids

The ancient Egyptians built pyramids as tombs for the pharaohs and their queens. Early pyramids were step pyramids, built as a series of platforms or steps. Later, the Egyptians developed a way of building incredibly high and smooth-sided pyramids. The pyramids were built using thousands of large stone blocks that were brought by boat along the Nile River or dragged across the desert from nearby **quarries**. The men who built the pyramids were

STEPS TO A PYRAMID
Pharaoh Djoser's step pyramid at Saqqara, completed in 2611 BC, was 204 feet (62 m) high, the largest building of its time.

paid workers and farmers who worked on them during the flood season when their fields were covered in water and they could not farm. The burial rooms within a pyramid were hidden at the end of long tunnels and passages. These were carefully blocked to protect their contents from thieves.

The Great Pyramid

The most well-known of these pyramids was built in 2550 BC for Pharaoh Khufu. It is known as the Great Pyramid and it was 481 feet (146 m) tall. When planning the pyramid, the **architects** designed it so that its sides faced directly north, south, east, and west. After marking the outline of the base in the sand, layers of blocks were built up one by one. After each layer was built, workers constructed sloping ramps made from mud bricks, chips of limestone rock, and clay. They used these ramps to help them drag the huge stones up high to build the next level. The pyramid took 20 years to build. When it was complete, workers covered it in blocks of white limestone, which were trimmed to give a smooth finish.

KHUFU'S PYRAMIDS

Alongside Khufu's pyramid were three pyramids for his queens, a temple where Khufu would be worshiped after he died, tombs for nobles, and other constructions.

Amazing Monuments

The pyramids are often noted as the largest ancient Egyptian monuments, but the pharaohs built many more spectacular constructions. Pharaohs often wanted to build something greater than the kings before them built. One pharaoh, Ramses II, even erased the names of previous pharaohs from monuments in Egypt to try to ensure only his name would be remembered.

Karnak

Karnak is a city of temples built by different ancient Egyptian pharaohs over a period of 2,000 years. It is dedicated to several gods, including Amun—one of the most powerful gods in ancient Egypt. It is the largest religious building ever made, covering about 250 acres (1 sq km). The Great Hypostyle Hall, at 54,000 square feet (5,017 sq m) and featuring 134 columns, is still the largest room of any religious building in the world.

The Great Sphinx

The Great Sphinx is a large, human-headed lion figure that is one of the world's largest statues, about 66 feet (20 m) tall and 240 feet (73 m) long. Its paws alone are twice the height of an adult man. The Sphinx was not built from separate blocks of stone, but carved from a single chunk of limestone rock that workers found when they were digging a quarry. Pharaoh Khafre, son of Khufu, ordered it to be built, and archaeologists believe that it represents Khafre.

THE GREAT SPHINX

The Great Sphinx sits to the south of Khafre's pyramid complex, found today at Giza near Cairo, Egypt.

Hatshepsut's Mortuary Temple

Hatshepsut built monuments in many sites, including **obelisks** and a palace at Karnak. Her mortuary temple at Luxor is one of the most beautiful of all the temples of ancient Egypt. It sits directly against the rock, which forms a natural amphitheater around it so that the temple seems to emerge from the rock. In the past, exotic trees and plants grew in a garden around it. Carvings in the temple tell stories of how Hatshepsut was related to the gods to confirm her right to be a pharaoh.

History in Hieroglyphs

Ancient Egyptians used a writing system called hieroglyphics, in which symbols and pictures represented sounds. The word "hieroglyph" means "language of the gods." Ancient Egyptians believed hieroglyphs were a gift from the gods that held magical powers. They carved these sacred symbols in stone on their temple walls, tombs, and other monuments.

How Hieroglyphs Work

The system of ancient Egyptian hieroglyphics uses more than 700 symbols and pictures. Some of the glyphs, or symbols, represent sounds, others represent objects or ideas. The Egyptians constructed words by using a combination of the two types. Egyptian hieroglyphs could be read from top to bottom, right to left, or left to right. Animal or bird symbols face the direction they are to be read. So, if a bird is facing left, the hieroglyphs should be read from left to right.

HIEROGLYPHS IN TOMBS
There are hieroglyphs and images of ancient Egyptian gods all over the walls of this tomb in Luxor.

Using Hieroglyphs

Hieroglyphs were difficult and time consuming to learn. Mainly only the royal family, priests, and government officials knew how to read and write them. Priests wrote prayers and texts in hieroglyphs related to life after death and worshiping the gods. Pharaohs ordered hieroglyphic stories about their lives and achievements to be carved into tomb walls. The pharaohs also ordered huge stone pillars, called obelisks, carved from a single piece of stone. They were covered with writings about the pharaohs and the gods so they would always be remembered.

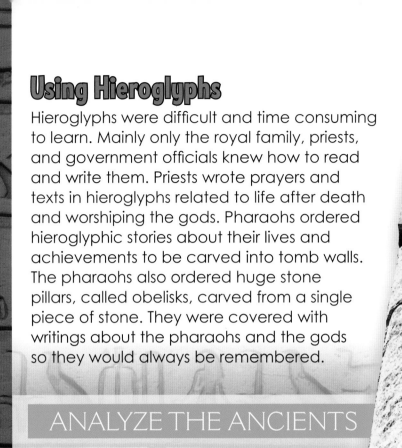

ANALYZE THE ANCIENTS

This is an ancient Egyptian obelisk. Use your knowledge to analyze the ancients and answer these questions.

1. Which way should we read the hieroglyphs on this obelisk? How do we know that, given that they can be written in different directions?

2. There are hieroglyphs on all four sides of an obelisk. Why do you think pharaohs had obelisks made?

CHAPTER 5

Work and Trade

Most ordinary Egyptians were farmers who worked the land. However, there were many other jobs to be done in ancient Egypt, too.

Farmers at Work

Ancient Egyptian famers grew a variety of crops in the fertile land around the Nile River. The Nile flooded over the land every year. Farmers waited until the waters went back down, then plowed the soil ready for sowing seeds. They used hand plows or larger plows that were pulled by oxen. Then they sowed seeds into the soil. They let pigs and other animals walk over the fields to help to push the seeds into the ground. To water their crops, they dug channels to carry water from the river to their fields. They also kept animals such as cows, sheep, goats, pigs, and ducks for their meat, milk, and skins, and to help with farming. They also grew nonfood crops such as flax, which was made into linen cloth.

PLOWING THE LAND
This painting of an ancient Egyptian farmer plowing with oxen was found in a tomb dating from 1200 BC.

Other Jobs

Some Egyptians worked as fishermen, or used their boats to carry people and goods up and down the river. Teachers were scribes or priests, who mainly taught the sons of royalty or wealthy families. Builders and laborers worked on the pyramids and other buildings. Designers and architects planned the buildings, and engineers figured out how to build them. Some people were entertainers such as dancers, singers, or musicians. Others were bakers, beer makers, or servants who looked after wealthy households and palaces. Doctors trained at schools called Houses of Life. Different doctors dealt with different problems, so there were eye doctors, dentists, head doctors, and stomach doctors. They made medicines from plants and animals. Surgeons stitched up and bandaged wounds, and broken legs were put in splints to keep them straight while they healed.

Arts and Crafts

Artists and craftsmen in ancient Egypt were usually trained and skilled laborers. They were often well respected in the community. They painted images in tombs, temples, and palaces, or on papyrus. They also made objects such as furniture and jewelry. Craftsmen with a particular skill worked in a workshop together. Craftsmen making objects for temples or the pharaoh worked in temple or palace workshops. Ordinary people bought objects for their homes from craftsmen in small local workshops.

Carpenters

Some craftsmen worked in workshops making furniture, mainly for the pharaoh and wealthy people. They used saws made of bronze to cut wood into blocks or lengths. Then, they shaped the blocks with tools such as chisels and adzes, which were like small axes. They often used special wood, such as ebony and cedar, to make furniture for the rich. Small decorative cabinets were made in which people could store their precious belongings.

TREASURE CHEST

This cedar wood box was made for King Tutankhamun's tomb. It has ivory knobs, wood carvings with gold and silver, and hieroglyphic inscriptions. Each leg is capped in silver, and inside are 16 different compartments.

Jewels of the Empire

Some ancient Egyptian craftsmen specialized in making jewelry of all kinds, including necklaces, bracelets, collars, and earrings. In a jewelry workshop, different people worked at different jobs, such as making beads, drilling holes in beads, and threading beads onto papyrus string. They often made jewelry for wealthy people out of glass, precious stones, and gold. Poor people wore jewelry made from painted clay, stones, shells, animal teeth, and bones. Jewelers had to learn the different and important meanings of particular stones, colors, and designs. For example, the precious gem turquoise was said to be a sacred stone that would bring good luck.

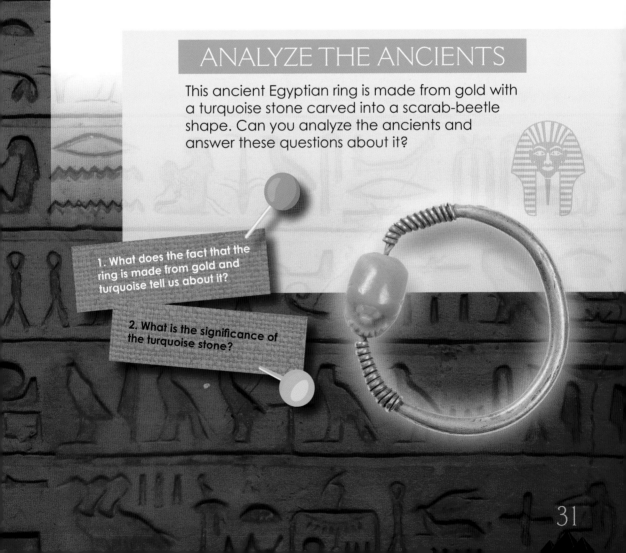

ANALYZE THE ANCIENTS

This ancient Egyptian ring is made from gold with a turquoise stone carved into a scarab-beetle shape. Can you analyze the ancients and answer these questions about it?

1. What does the fact that the ring is made from gold and turquoise tell us about it?

2. What is the significance of the turquoise stone?

Buying and Selling

Ancient Egyptians had a variety of goods that were bought from and sold to other countries. Lapis lazuli, a blue gemstone from Afghanistan, has been found in Egyptian tombs. Pieces of Egyptian pottery have been found as far away as Knossos in Crete, near Greece.

Imports and Exports

The location of Egypt's waterways helped trade between Europe, Africa, and Asia. The ancient Egyptians **exported** grain when the harvest was so good that they had enough to spare. They also exported decorative objects such as stone and pottery vases, linen, papyrus, gold vessels, ox skins, ropes, and dried fish. They traded these items in return for goods not commonly found in Egypt. Horses, cattle, silver, copper, and valuable minerals came from Syria and Palestine. Turquoise came from Sinai. From Cyprus, they bought copper and ivory, and gold came from the mines of eastern Nubia. Products such as **incense**, and wood such as cedar, juniper, and ebony, were **imported** from western Asia and Africa.

GOING TO MARKET
This model from ancient Egypt shows people carrying goods to or from a market.

32

Merchants and Markets

Boats and barges carried goods up and down the Nile River between different cities and beyond. The sea route began on the Nile at the port of Memphis. Once goods were unloaded, they were hauled to different cities and merchants by camel, donkey, cart, or on foot. The ancient Egyptians bought goods from merchants at markets, and traded their own goods through shops and in the public marketplaces. In the marketplace, stone weights known as deben weights were used to calculate the value of grain and other objects that were to be exchanged. Later, around 400 BC, gold, silver, and bronze coins were used in Egypt. But, even then, bartering or exchanging goods was still popular.

CHAPTER 6

Everyday Life

The kind of life you would have lived in ancient Egypt depended on whether you were rich or poor, and a man or a woman.

At Home

Whether you were a pharaoh or a farmer, most people's homes were made from mud bricks. Mud was mixed with straw and water, then sun-dried in wooden molds to make bricks. Mud bricks kept homes cool.

Ordinary people lived in homes with a few rooms, often within a walled courtyard. Stairs led up to a flat roof where people could sleep when it was too hot inside. Clay pots were used as food containers, and baskets were made from reeds and date palm leaves.

The pharaoh's palace belonged to a complex of many buildings, including temples and buildings where priests lived. Beautiful gardens were tended by slaves or servants.

A MODEL FAMILY

Family was important to the ancient Egyptians. They often had statues or models made of themselves with their children.

The pharaoh and nobles hunted a variety of wild animals, including bulls, antelopes, hippopotamuses, elephants, and lions.

Men and Women

The pharaoh and nobles had a lot of free time. The men enjoyed fishing or going hunting for wild ducks in the marshes. Wealthy women are shown in tomb paintings sitting on couches talking to each other, playing games, and listening to music. In working families, the men worked outside the home, growing food or earning grain to feed their families. Women ran the household, cooking, cleaning, making clothes, and caring for the children. Sons, and sometimes daughters, of rich families went to school, where they learned reading, writing, and math. Other boys and girls stayed with their parents. Girls were taught by their mothers to look after the home, while boys learned their father's trade. Some women had a trade or owned a business, and earned their own money. Their daughters could learn to run a business, too.

Feasts and Food

Tomb paintings provide a lot of valuable archaeological evidence about how the ancient Egyptians lived and what foods they ate. The meals eaten by rich and poor were often quite different.

Food from the Land

Farms provided a range of vegetables and fruits that could be enjoyed by rich and poor. Farmers grew onions, garlic, leeks, beans, lentils, peas, radishes, cabbages, cucumbers, and lettuce. They grew corn and wheat that were made into bread. They grew barley that was made into beer. Grains were harvested and stored in special buildings for later use. Ancient Egyptians also grew fruits such as dates, figs, pomegranates, melons, and grapes. They collected honey to sweeten their food. They even sweetened their breads with dates, honey, and figs. Meals were served in pottery bowls. Ancient Egyptians used knives to cut food up, but they did not eat with knives and forks.

FOOD FOR A FEAST
This ancient Egyptian painting shows large quantities of food ready for a feast.

36

Rich and Poor

Many tombs have paintings of royals and wealthy people at banquets. At these feasts, they ate foods such as roast oxen, pork, and birds such as duck. They also drank wine. They used a variety of spices and flavorings, including mustard, salt, cumin, coriander, honey, dill, and vinegar, so their food was probably quite tasty. Ordinary people would only have eaten red meat on very special occasions because they could not afford it. They ate lentils instead, and used a hook and line or nets to catch fish to eat. They often dried fish in the sunshine so they could eat it without cooking. They also soaked some fish in salty water to store it for later. Ancient Egyptians hunted wild animals and trapped birds for meat, which they boiled or roasted. The poor ate lots of bread and drank water, milk, or beer. However, the beer was thick, and the bread was gritty because the wheat it was made from was ground with a stone.

Ancient Egyptian Style

The ancient Egyptians thought keeping clean and caring about the way they looked was very important. People who looked scruffy were looked down on.

What to Wear

Both men and women wore linen clothing made of fabric woven from flax. It was usually undyed, so most clothes were cream colored. Men wore short skirts made from a rectangular piece of linen folded around the body and tied at the waist. Sometimes, they also wore tunics. Women wore long dresses. Better-quality linen was used for rich people's robes, which often had decorative panels. Rich men and women added more color to their outfits with beads, bracelets, armlets, and necklaces. They often added colorful capes and shawls. Most people went barefoot, though some wore sandals made of papyrus or leather.

DRESSING LIKE NOBLES
This image of a royal couple walking in a garden shows the decorative clothing worn by the rich ancient Egyptians.

Making It Up

The other distinctive thing about ancient Egyptian style is that everyone wore kohl. Kohl is a dark-colored cosmetic that the Egyptians made by grinding up stones. They mixed this powder with water or oil to make a paste. They often drew thick bands of black kohl above their eyes and green kohl below their eyes. Kohl was applied with their fingers or with a tool called a kohl stick. The thick eye paint acted like an ancient form of sunglasses. It helped protect their eyes by absorbing some of the sun's glare. The shape of the kohl lines probably also represented the Eye of Horus, which was an important symbol of protection, royal power, and good health.

ANALYZE THE ANCIENTS

This death mask from an ancient Egyptian tomb was made in the likeness of a woman. Using information you have learned, can you answer these questions about it?

1. How did the kohl around their eyes help the ancient Egyptians cope with the hot, sunny weather?

2. How is the shape of the kohl lines connected to ancient Egyptian religion?

Games and Entertainment

The ancient Egyptians enjoyed a variety of games and forms of entertainment in their free time. Pharaohs and nobles often organized competitions and awarded prizes to the winners.

Active Games

Some of the physical sports men competed in included archery, wrestling, boxing, long jump, weight lifting, and stick fighting. Men and women went swimming, and men ran long-distance races to show off their physical fitness. People also played other games that are similar to games we play today. One game was a type of field hockey. It was played with bats made from palm tree branches and a ball made of squashed up papyrus fiber. The bats were bent at the end like hockey sticks.

Board Games

The ancient Egyptians liked to play board games. The most popular was Senet. This was a game for two people, played on a board of 30 squares divided into three rows of ten squares each. An elaborately carved and decorated Senet board was found in Tutankhamen's tomb, but people could also play it on a grid scratched into the dirt. The number or type of moves people could play was often decided using throw sticks or animal bones.

SENET BOARD

Archaeologists are not sure how Senet was played, although they suspect it had a religious significance. However, they do know that people played it using an early form of dice.

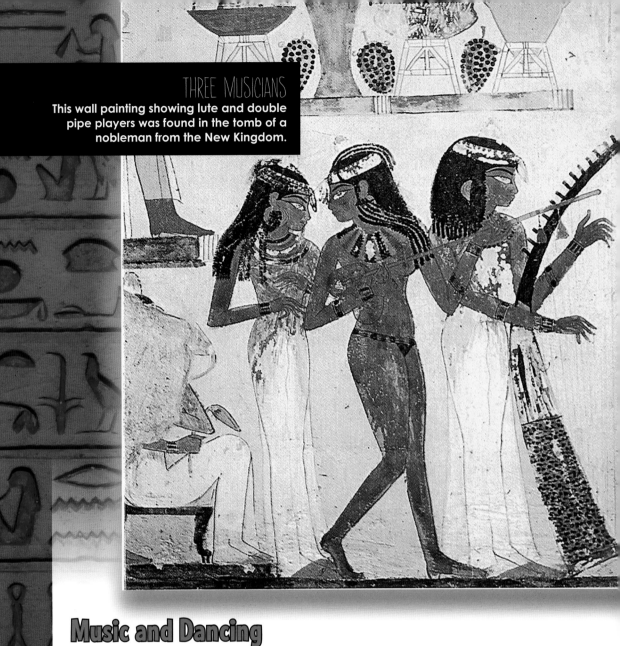

THREE MUSICIANS

This wall painting showing lute and double pipe players was found in the tomb of a nobleman from the New Kingdom.

Music and Dancing

Many paintings on tomb walls do not show the guests dancing at a banquet. Instead, the guests watch trained musicians and dancers performing. During the New Kingdom, it appears that most of the musicians may have been women. One of the oldest instruments was a flute made of reed or wood. Gradually, musicians used a wide variety of different instruments, including harps, lutes, flutes, oboes, tambourines, seven-stringed harp-like lyres, and rattles.

The End of Ancient Egypt

At the peak of ancient Egypt, the Egyptians ruled an area that extended from what is now Sudan in the south to the edge of modern Turkey in the north. So why did the civilization finally come to an end? This is a complicated question to answer, but it probably happened for a variety of reasons.

A Tale of Decline

Ancient Egypt began to lose its ability to win battles because it lacked certain natural **resources**. While other empires around Egypt were expanding by conquering people using weapons made from iron, ancient Egypt did not have the resources to make that metal, so it became vulnerable to competing armies. A **civil war** between different parts of ancient Egypt led to a north-south divide. Being no longer united also meant the country was more at risk from large invading armies. Ancient Egypt was also struggling for money. The pharaoh, priests, and nobles held onto most of the wealth and the cost of war was increasing. Bigger armies also meant more mouths to feed, and this put a strain on the farms.

ATTACK FROM THE ASSYRIANS

This is a carving of an Assyrian warship. Shields protect the side, and a pointed ram at the front was used to spilt open and sink enemy ships.

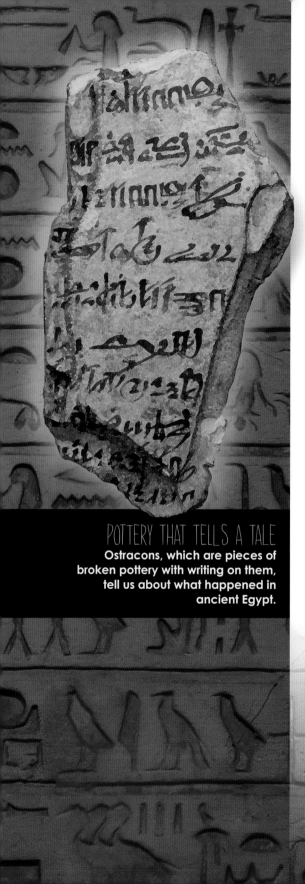

POTTERY THAT TELLS A TALE
Ostracons, which are pieces of broken pottery with writing on them, tell us about what happened in ancient Egypt.

Climate Problems

Toward the end of the ancient Egyptian civilization, the climate also had an impact. Low rainfall caused the water level in the Nile to fall. A period of time in which the weather became colder and drier reduced the harvest, and many people died from starvation (a lack of food) or dehydration (a lack of water). Later, there was also a period of especially heavy flooding, when the river's waters overflowed at unusual times and ruined fields of crops, causing more hunger and death.

Invasions

Ancient Egypt was greatly weakened by these events, and soon its land was being taken by invaders. For example, the Libyans invaded several times, Assyrians attacked around 671 BC, and Persia invaded sometime later. In 332 BC, Alexander the Great conquered Egypt as part of his takeover of the Persian Empire. This helped bring an end to the Egyptian way of life.

Answers

Did you manage to analyze the ancients? Check your answers against the correct answers on these pages.

PAGE 9

1. The fact that the object is made of gold and was found in a large, secret tomb shows that it belonged to a pharaoh.
2. The symbol of a cobra goddess was used by pharaohs who believed the goddess would protect them by spitting flames at their enemies.

PAGE 15

1. The soldiers are the lowest rank. They were foot soldiers, perhaps farmers forced to join the army for a battle.
2. The soldiers are shown with weapons and ready for an attack because Egypt was probably under threat from an enemy at the time, rather than enjoying a time of peace.

PAGE 19

1. The symbol on the amulet on page 19 is of the Eye of Horus, which is a symbol of good health. Ancient Egyptians believed that it had powers to keep them well.
2. The amulet is made from turquoise, a stone the ancient Egyptians believed would protect them from wounds and attack.

PAGE 27

1. To read the hieroglyphs on the obelisk in the right direction, we have to see which way the bird or animal symbols are facing. Here, they are facing left, so the hieroglyphs should be read from left to right.
2. Pharaohs had obelisks made and covered in hieroglyphs about themselves and the gods, so that they and their achievements would always be remembered.

PAGE 31

1. The fact the ring is made of gold and the precious gem turquoise suggests it was worn by a wealthy person. Poor people wore jewelry made from painted clay, stones, shells, animal teeth, and bones.
2. The significance of turquoise is that ancient Egyptians believed it was a sacred stone that would bring them good luck.

PAGE 39

1. Thick, dark bands of kohl around the ancient Egyptians' eyes absorbed some of the sun's glare. It worked like an ancient form of sunglasses to help protect their eyes.
2. The shape of the kohl lines was thought to represent the Eye of Horus. This was an important symbol of protection, royal power, and good health.

Glossary

afterlife life after death

archaeologists people who study artifacts to learn about how people lived in the past

architects people who design and plan buildings

civil war war between two parts of the same country

civilization a settled and stable community in which people live together peacefully and use systems such as writing to communicate

cultures the beliefs, customs, and arts of a particular group of people or country

dynasty a family that rules a country for a long time by passing control from parent to child, usually father to son

embalming treating a dead body to keep it from decaying

empire a large area of land or group of countries ruled by one leader

exported taken out of one country and sold to another country

fertile describes soil that is full of nutrients so plants grow well in it

imported bought and brought in from another country

incense a substance burned to give off a pleasant smell, often used in religious rituals

inherited got from their parents

kingdom a single area ruled over by a king or queen

monuments statues, buildings, or other structures made to remember an event, a time, or a person

mummification a way to preserve a dead body by treating it with oils and wrapping it in strips of cloth

nobles people of the highest class in certain societies

obelisks tall stone pillars, which are square or rectangular at the base and become narrower toward the top; used as monuments

offerings things that people give as part of a religious ceremony or ritual

quarries deep pits from which stone for building is dug

rank position of importance in an army or other group

resin a sticky substance produced by trees

resources things that can be used or made into new things, such as water and rock

rituals religious ceremonies

slaves people who are owned by other people and have to obey them

temples buildings where people go to worship their god or gods

tomb a building where a dead person is put to rest

Books

Drimmer, Stephanie Warren. *National Geographic Kids Readers: Ancient Egypt.* Washington, D.C.: National Geographic Children's Books, 2018.

Hart, George. *Ancient Egypt* (DK Eyewitness). New York, NY: DK Eyewitness Books, 2014.

Randolph, Joanne. *Living and Working in Ancient Egypt* (Back in Time). New York, NY: Enslow Publishing, 2017.

Rodger, Ellen. *Ancient Egypt Inside Out* (Ancient Worlds Inside Out). St. Catharines, ON: Crabtree Publishing Company, 2017.

Websites

Find more information about ancient Egypt at:
www.dkfindout.com/uk/history/ancient-egypt

Discover incredible facts about ancient Egypt at:
www.natgeokids.com/uk/discover/history/egypt/ten-facts-about-ancient-egypt

Learn about some amazing ancient Egyptian inventions at:
science.howstuffworks.com/innovation/inventions/5-amazing-ancient-egyptian-inventions.htm

Publisher's note to educators and parents: Our editors have carefully reviewed these websites to ensure that they are suitable for students. Many websites change frequently, however, and we cannot guarantee that a site's future contents will continue to meet our high standards of quality and educational value. Be advised that students should be closely supervised whenever they access the Internet.

Index